The Tortoise of History

The Tortoise of History

poems by Anselm Hollo

COFFEE HOUSE PRESS
MINNEAPOLIS
2016

Coffee House Press books are available to the trade through our primary distribu-tor, Consortium Book Sales & Distribution, cbsd.com or (800) 283-3572. For per-sonal orders, catalogs, or other information, write to info@coffeehousepress.org.

Coffee House Press is a nonprofit literary publishing house. Support from pri-vate foundations, corporate giving programs, government programs, and gener-ous individuals helps make the publication of our books possible. We gratefully acknowledge their support in detail in the back of this book.

LIBRARY OF CONGRESS CATALOGING-IN-PUBLICATION DATA

Names: Hollo, Anselm, author.
Title: The tortoise of history / Anselm Hollo.
Description: Minneapolis : Coffee House Press, [2016]
Identifiers: LCCN 2015039024 | ISBN 9781566894449
    (softcover)
Subjects: | BISAC: POETRY / American / General. | POETRY /
    Continental European.
Classification: LCC PR6015.O415 A6 2016 | DDC 821/.914—dc23
LC record available at http://lccn.loc.gov/2015039024

ACKNOWLEDGMENTS

Some of these works have appeared in *Beatitude* (San Francisco), *Big Bridge, Burp, Café Review, Gerry Mulligan, Golden Handcuffs Review, halfcircle* (Oxford, UK), *Square One, Thuggery and Grace, Van Gogh's Ear* (Paris, France), *Vanitas* (New York City), *Woodland Pattern Broadsides* (Milwaukee), and *Yawp* (New Orleans). The author is grateful to the editors, publishers, printers, and dis-tributors of these publications.

Deep appreciation to the Civitella Ranieri Foundation, which honored Anselm with a Fellowship in 2005, and with which he wrote "At Civitella Ranieri."

Special thanks to David Beaudouin, who first published my version of the fragments of Hipponax on his Tropos Press (Hipponax of Ephesus, Baltimore, MD, 1995).

PRINTED IN THE UNITED STATES OF AMERICA
23 22 21 20 19 18 17 16   1 2 3 4 5 6 7 8

For Janey, to the end of time

Contents

Foreword

Could Anselm have possibly foretold
that *The Tortoise of History,* this peculiar compilation of old and new
musings, revisitations, letters to past and future, love notes
    to friends—and to me

was an inevitable foreshadowing of *this* day, when I, *his* Janey
would stop the endless fuss, unplug the phone, sit quietly
    for 20 minutes,

and then settle into *his* chair, in *our* kitchen
and read *this* book—aloud, in *his* cadence
and *really* take in

this "message in a bottle"?

—Jane Dalrymple-Hollo

The Tortoise of History

PART 1

The Tortoise of History

Wildly Tangled

wildly tangled dream:
festivities
with current presidente
quite a nice guy really

old face old cat in mail

wind drives propaganda
so   have a last capitalist
cigarette
in this lame old plutocracy

everybody
seems quite happily occupied
by their precious little lives

but She Who Must Be Obeyed
She Who Laughs at Your Jokes

love them both as one
as best you can

Quake

The ocean sure is a BIG tub

the continents
                                none too solid

they growl!

                        TECTONIC GRIND

"say something?"

LA TERRA TREMA

but not right here
not right now

I love your hair
                                atop your dancer's body

absolute loveliness
                                in a quaking world

Don't Tell Me

Don't tell me you can't
love the dead
sometimes I love the dead more
than the still living

there was a time
one sounded as
"authoritative"
as any so-called media

(in my case
shortwave radio person
for ten cold war years)

and they all
old amigos
young apprentices
do still sound that way

not the same but

                    just that way

Why Not

put the book mark
at the wrong page

She Said

Don't fret   she said
it's all right

a human
is not a machine

Art History

Someone comes along
gives that tedious old thing
a new twist   or
breaks its neck

the old questions
don't change:

what do you want me to say?
what do you want me to do?

Home

For jdh

When we drove across
all those states
away from your old hometown
and you were crying

for good reason
(familiar familial strife)
I tried to console you
and worried about how to do that

until I thought I knew
and told you we're going home now
even though then
we had no idea
where home really would be

Some Ways

Some ways you know more
than ever before

some ways
it has become

even harder
to convey that increase

City Of

City OF, says Alice
that's what they all are, the cities
OF
they're OF
OF pain OF love OF life OF hurt OF dying
OF memory   ach   yes   OF mamma mia

"Why Read So Much?"

Why read
so much?

to see
what others

may have
found out

and we
would not

want to
miss

before
we die

Time

Too slow
when you're
not here

Dasein

Lightness, my foot—
the incredible ONSLAUGHT of being!

feeling floaty
all right as long as
it's a "controlled" float

but what if it isn't?
reading Marx and Spinoza
dust to dust
you soon will be too

life in the folds
which do not unfold
contradictions
nothing but

"an exhibition of REAL HUMAN BODIES"
i.e., plastinated corpses

it is hard to please the dead

old man looking for his youth
in another
very different body

"Desire?"
"Where do we stand on desire?"

"We don't stand
we just sit
or lie down
dreaming"

(quietly screaming
in our sleep)

Somewhere

Between the cat and the tree
     must be my country

and the finch
     singing above us

about the world
     that suffers
          and yearns

Who Said He Could Do This

Half a century trying
      still not sure why
            he ties his shoelaces funny

Boulder, Colorado

"That's such *inappropriate* behavior"
   —woman in antique shop
         to small white terrier

   after it charged outside
      to bark at
            big Labrador

"There Is Room in the Room That I Room In"

Said (I believe) Ted Berrigan
    and there is room
        in the rooms that we room in

for work and works
    of art
        and of course myriad objects

needed and/or believed to be so
    and talk and touch and looks
        there is room for us

who may feel large sometimes
    if not downright great
        but also truly quite small

        as I told you one night

Who Would Have Thought—
Santa Ganesh!

Lovely Parvati's par-
thenogenetic son
bravely guards
the door to her bath

gets his head lopped
by angry Shiva
always angry
but now repentant

replaces lost head
with an elephant's—
yes Virginia there is a
Santa Claus

but here's a Santa Ganesh:
his ride is a mouse
not an eight-legged horse
or sled pulled by reindeer

his gifts open doors
through mind and illusion
> in heads and bodies
> ever refreshed

> so hail to the Universe
> ever refreshed

100-Year-Old Poet

Modigliani
        first name Amedeo
                didn't live long enough
to paint you
        this morning
                (or one of many mornings)
stretched out
        beside me
                to tell the truth, he, Amedeo

did not live long enough at all
        to meet & paint you
                but Hollo (first name Anselm)

has lived long enough
        to see you there
                unfortunately

he is not a great painter
        but he is
                your 100-year-old poet

Nothing

nothing is too
        unimportant
                to write about

nothing is too
        important
                to write about

there really is
        nothing
                to write about

except for
        you
                over there

Rides with Bob Creeley

"The man who really knows
can tell all that is transmissible
in a very few words"
—SAID OLD EZ

Young Bob's few words hit home oh did they ever
        plain and ironic
            always aware
     how insecure
words' ground can be

     both noir and humane

light flashing through dark trees
               by the side of the road

mind & heart stop for a fraction
        time slows

then Thelonious
     strikes the next note
     and the next

and you wonder how you could ever not
            have known that
     this would be
               the next word
unexpected yet perfect

but you didn't know
     or you forgot

and the poem takes you
to a love of the kind wisdom

refuses to abandon
    the endlessly
    contradictory
    human heart

    for grand abstractions

so we make it through hours of talk
    and laughter and blizzards
on our way on the road
    heading east to the rising sun

to rescue she who walks into the sea

before the waters close above her

a tall woman
              but not that tall

    and then we all trudge back
    to the General Store
    for some terrible coffee

Bugs Killed Our Tree

bugs killed our tree

The Less Known

Always thought of d'Artagnan
as the little guy
                         can change the gears
                                                          of history
If even just a tad
with a little help from his friends

well   how true can that be
this is not unimportant

guess we were
                         a wee bit aroused
seeing those guys jump around fighting
        with long knives which is   what the Cheyenne & Lakota

called Custer's cavalry

Yes Custer wore his hair Mousquetaire fashion as did

Cody Hickok Omohundro

            & the less known
                         Rocky Mountain Joe

Rainy Night

Missing and losing

More ancient than loving

Animal Time
                          so short

         never
         enough

Ah, let it come down

New Year's Poem

Cats
are wiser
than humans

especially present
human chieftains

so here's wishing you

cat wisdom
up
(note:
NOT down)
the years

including the one
coming up

Crocus

Hello yellow
crocus she says
snaps a picture   looks away   turns to see
the deer that later swallows the crocus
oh well   Spring
will spring

More So Than Before

Love the cluster of Johnny-Jump-Ups in front of my green house

love the words chalked on a pillar
of the university's library:

> TO YOUR POCKET I WOULD SCURRY
> IF THE COLD RAIN FELL AND SHRANK ME SMALL

no idea if that's a quote from popular song
or children's book
or spontaneous anonymous ejaculation
to the unknown muse

but hey it's hard not to feel that it's got something
same something those Johnny-Jump-Ups
sitting atop a crack in the pavement got

which is really all
the scribe of these lines is doing too

sitting atop a crack in the pavement
brought out and sustained by sun and rain

and if you think that's too sweet, well, not to worry
bitter antidotes are easy to find

Broken Flowers

See her sleep
feel no crazy

pack obsession
DA!   what?

not phone wildly
          or oligarchly
just un poco company

just go feel forever
before the dark

anyone home?
old cat in snow

wind drives molecules—
you the ones?

this me years ago
says the cigarette

lame old prick
          blurs into hills
light has brushed

poetic, what?

un poco cheek
rest desert flame on moss

or shyly dream
inspiring tufts

drummer, remember

African Gray Parrot with a Brain the Size of a Walnut Understands a Numerical Concept Akin to Zero

Yes my dear that may well be true
but I do wish
this pleasant early June evening breeze
would evaporate
all the terrible servants of Mammon
masquerading as servants of the "American People"—
in a kind of reverse "rapture," i.e.,

tomorrow morning they just wouldn't BE here anymore

Ah it is late
in the game dear hearts
dear hearts it is late in the game

and how will the untold be told?

will the bugs remember?

or in a dog's or cat's brain a small flicker
        that there were these "humans" once

no no says the Doge of Dogs
no no says the Caesar of Cats

no   to quote your great singer Tom Lehrer
"We'll all go together when we go"

Listen to the Long Hiss of Time

Given a functional
                    time-reverse machine
who wouldn't mind
                    a second childhood

One would be better equipped
                              to deal with one's parents
but being a poet it's hard
                    to imagine this society
that wouldn't think one
                    a parasite
or as archaic as
          let's say a "mule skinner"

The Way They Pop Up Now

late in this life
the dead and the living

Technicolor
or black and white

different parts of the brain
begin talking to each other

small children reappear
and now they're either dead

or alive as film directors
record producers high tech designers

but some ancients are still present too
even more ancient than this brain life

looks out the window
thinks squirrels are not very contemplative

but the cats watching them are

Mirlitonnade

fous qui disiez
plus jamais
vite
redites
                    (Samuel Beckett)

you fools who said
never again
hurry
say it again

A Valentine

Love
play a song
for jaguar
and tree

and you and me
and all that lives
and loves
to be

"Growing Old Together"

To Nathaniel Tarn on his 80th

Came to the Empire
        got to know and love many
                of its inhabitants

watched it being
        at least some of the time
                what it claimed to be

now old
        we feel privileged to watch
                its waning

The Bugs Sang Grand

"The bugs sang grand"
—CHARLES OLSON, *MAXIMUS II.8*

You're not Billie Holiday
you look a bit like Billie Holiday

but you don't really sound like Billie Holiday
so   what are we supposed to do about you?

a "fresh" face   an old face
a face familiar   from back and beyond

(well, I thought that
so I guess I have a right to say it)

"mistaken identity" "amnesia"
good old noir plots

smoke rises

on earth
smoke rises

the untold stories
the untellable ones

You Were Talking (1967)

"You were talking
talking
not looking at me at all"

ephemeral light effects
lack of oxygen in the brain
other space travel symptoms

the doll
back from the "Doctor's"
with a new head
"it is not the same"

I had been away
where no one could know who I was

your eyes
coiling my mind
back into my head

The Pika

So aren't we all
the trembling fawn
or baby rat

entering
re-entering
this terrifying place

so place is it
but time is it too

deceptive results
of efforts to extend
what we believe are our senses

the Pika
can only live
above 6,000 feet

it does not know
any better place

75

It ain't the middle of life
    but I'm still
        lost in the woods

Formal Prosody

Never ever needed
more formal prosody
than what Thelonious
teaches

and as it goes on
it just needs more
of that
rapt attention

The Stars

The stars
do not
"blink out"

oh no   it's UP
they puff
quite monstrously

and then

they EXPLODE

As

The music
goes on
as long as
you can stand it

A Place Is a While

Over there up
                               on the hillside
walking uphill
in the dark

anything rather than nothing

little lost homesteaders on this web

there is room in this room that we room in

myriad objects

the Poet and the Centipede

a place is a place

a place is a while

After They've Gone

yes

yes

yes

       we spoke of

              you

              & you

              & you

              & you

Still

Still as alive as the pygmy hippo
in the Liberian forests of the night

but shall end up owing many
letters to the dead

Reading Joanne Kyger

Such poems
    of gentle sadness

not the sadness
    that makes you want to burrow
    into the ground
    jump off a tall building
    slit your wrists

        no not that kind
        but one of gentle rain
            falling
            softly
        on memory gardens
            in your brain

Hunchback Mountain

Small caves in the mountains
not much time left to find them

not enough lifeboats
20 hours
until the fish start to eat us

all right let's go to heaven BEFORE we die
the rich will always be with us

indulging in the usual
religious rape & pillage

the prophets a figment of bad imagination
and love a labor indeed

of having to shovel
the loveless out of the way

all right let's go to heaven
BEFORE we die

"Twenty hours until the fish started to eat us"
—Egyptian ferry disaster survivor

Late Night, Old Surprises

Doctor Faustus sits in his kitchen
facing Black Feline Angel
on the opposite stool
who looks at him, sends telepathic message:

"No, old friend, you're really not Dr. Faustus
and I'm not Mephistopheles
and you don't really want to be Richard Burton, do you?
Nor do you want her to be Liz Taylor—do you?"

all right, I say
all right, old friend
(she does not look like Liz at all
but just enchantingly herself)

never mind, I say, us oldies
just have to hang on
to our lives
and true loves, too

Noir

Dream dreams dream
dream dreams a samba perennial

you me him her
"Staples beginning to rust in otherwise fine copy"

the back of the electric fan's head
looks like a Wyndham Lewis

but "God" does not look like a Wyndham Lewis
"God" does not look like anything at all

> (god
> & dog
> don't
> vote)

Hunter Thompson said he was a
"road man for the Lords of Karma"

"He stomped Terra" said his son

Oh it makes an ill musick la vida
and only lasts a pissing-while

Running

Running
                    to meet
running
                    away

that's what we do

Sitting in Peaceful Lamplight

reading a book on how to become a better person

Zophiel the cat touches my leg and asks me

"Why don't you write a book about becoming just a pretty good person

& by the way what happened to my late-night snack?"

At Civitella Ranieri

To rise out of the mist each morning
into a version of *The Peaceable Kingdom*

feeling as dumbly content as Mr. Hicks's lions
for the first hour or two, and then

to confront the beauty of Umbria
and person—correction: persons—all
concerned with improving
the intelligence of the species
of ape we are—

      is a gift and delight that occurs
      in few civitellas of this planet

this planet—such as it is now,
still struggling on,
trying to leave a record

perhaps no more permanent than the head
now lost   of Ruggiero Cane,
("Khan" = Condottiere)
who returned from his wars
to rebuild castle and fiefdom

      later resuscitated—
      and truly renewed—by Ursula,
      saintly person, whose love still sustains us

      here—among persons
      of light and delight

The Bard of the Pyrenees

Young poet Raoul Lafagette
arrives from the provinces
like a latter-day d'Artagnan
bearing letters of introduction
to important persons
among others the Democratic Deputy Eugène Pelletan
and the poet Théophile Gautier

On hearing of manuscript verses
the democratic deputy favors his visitor with a résumé
of his views on human progress:
"Why do you write in VERSE?
No one cares for it now. It is little read, and not at all sold.
In the childhood of humanity
verse had its raison d'être.
The first songs are hymns, outbursts of terror
or of enthusiasm. But in our age
of SKEPTICAL MATURITY
and republican independence
verse
is a superannuated form. We prefer
PROSE,
which by virtue of its freedom of movement
accords more truly
with the instincts of democracy."

Whereupon followed a demonstration
of the same principles
from the spectacle of external nature,
in which the crystal is the type of the poem's line
and "the masterpiece which dominates this hierarchy"
—woman—with her undulating grace
is the analogue of prose.

Young Lafagette, enlightened but unconvinced, does not
tear up his manuscripts,
but carries them a few days afterward
with a letter of introduction from GEORGE SAND
to the house of THÉOPHILE GAUTIER

author of the exquisite
ENAMELS AND CAMEOS
who receives the young man with paternal kindness
but after reading the two pieces of verse
submitted to him by the neophyte
speaks as follows: "Your verses
are 40 years older than yourself. They are
too old, therefore—
that is to say, too young.
Poets sang in this manner in 1830. NOWADAYS
we desire a more compressed, more concrete poetry.
Lamartine was a sublime bard,
but his vague effusions are no longer
to our taste. Musset is a great poet
but an exceedingly bad model.
Read HUGO much, he is the true master."

"And Théophile Gautier?" timidly murmurs
   the visitor. "And me, too, a little,
   if it pleases you to think so," replies Gautier,
   smiling. "You are a poet
   and must not abandon poetry. Only I advise you
   to make three or four thousand verses
   and before you publish anything
   burn them."

Note: Raoul Lafagette (1842–1913) returned to the French Pyrenees and
pursued the advice of both interlocutors. In front of the town of Foix's
mayoral offices stands on a plinth a marble bust with the inscription
"Raoul Lafagette, Bard of the Pyrenees."

See What You Got, Tomorrow (2002)

If it's not propaganda, what is it?
If it's not brainwashing, what is it?
If it's not a capitalist plutocracy, what is it?
The politics universally incorrect

Catnip   yes it nips the old cat &
"How will anyone understand those poems of yours
Unless they're stoned?"
A crazy princess asked me twenty years ago

This is the phase of early a.m. phone calls
Observing this, I am
What a dumbo flap flap dark peacocks rise in the wind
Home at three a.m. from eight hours

Proofreading offshore contracts   (San Fran '81)
Drank myself to sleep feeling lonely as shit
Then even more so
This ain't funny not funny enough

How to stay funny enough back then
Not even a fish for company back then
A sad sack for sure
Let's just go out and die under the stars

In the snow
Driven by these little molecules
Rilke molecules Billy Yeats molecules
Yes I had a son whose molecules gave out before mine

I was not good to him   Not good for him
He was as they say hard to take
Once tried to kill me and the feeling was mutual
So did my "folks" and that feeling was mutual too

So now I am grateful for kindness
So now I try to understand power
You help to keep this network thriving says the radio
And some of the poor sons of bitches

Out there are creating a terrible beauty
Some of them ready to kill for their "god"
In a persistent drunken trance
Wishing to live forever

But not here and now
Are you asleep are you alone
And the cigarettes keep jumping out of the pack
Life a Riemann bottle:

Can't get in can't get out
Estrange it Estrange it
Yeah fill 'er up Jack lessgo
Gosh yes the music does tinkle on

(Bertolt Brecht:)

And the ones
They stand in darkness
And the others
In the light

The ones well lit
Oh yes we see them
The ones in darkness
We do not see

Looking at the Old Hand

For Simon Pettet

looking at the old hand
        I almost lost and
                its old bones and veins

I print your messages
        dear friends
                and feel the love and

accept it with
        all my heart and brain which
                still feel like they're working

Two Strange Little Vessels

one a tiny wooden chest from the once-upon-a-time
small town of Hameln

whence the Pied Piper of Hamelin
was said to have lured all the town's rodents away
by playing a magical tune on his pipes

but sadly the town's children heard it too
and followed the Piper where?
nobody knows for sure

      the other a small bowl with what looks like an Etruscan design
      of two birds identical except for their coloration
      (I'm sure it is not "genuinely" Etruscan)

        and,   and a small
        nonallergenic
        metal flower
        complete with roots

it is a garlic flower

for healing

provenance unknown

AND a small book from Crown Point

Press of some etchings

by the late

Mr. John Cage

HAPPY BIRTHDAY JANEY!!!!

James Butler A.K.A. Wild Bill Hickok's Final
Stream of Consciousness

holy shit i shouldn't have had that big shot of whiskey but what the
hell i'll just sit down here with my back to the bar this is just a half-
assed mining camp "deadwood" give me a break i survived chicago
new york and that crazy buffalo bill and his buddy buntline and their
goddamn wild west shows ... .. .

Blue Moon

Being dead, Steve Carey, wonderful poet
can't sign his *Selected Poems*
to   me

These days I find myself
ordering only books by poets
who are

being
dead

Another One Gone Too Soon

"Like RIVETS"
said Ken Smith
about my lines

don't know if
he really approved

but now it's
way too late
to ask him

2010 A Spring of Departures

Would you mind
                    POPPING UP
                                        again?

You can't just
              disappear
                                    or can you?

The Tortoise of History

The tortoise of history
keeps stomping along

it carries
on its back

all the prophets,
visionaries,
"great men"

It is almost blind

but its legs still work

PART 2

Hipponax, His Poems

"I ain't got no future, but Lord, Lord, what a past."
—BILLIE HOLIDAY, AS QUOTED BY GEORGE MELLY

William Carlos Williams ends Book 1 of his *Paterson* (New Directions 1992, p. 40) with a quote from John Addington Symonds's two-volume *Studies of the Greek Poets,* prefacing it with an "N.B.":

"In order apparently to bring the meter still more within the sphere of prose and common speech, Hipponax ended his iambics with a spondee or a trochee instead of an iambus, doing thus the utmost violence to the rhythmical structure. These deformed and mutilated verses were called *choliambi,* lame or limping iambics. They communicated a curious crustiness to the style. These *choliambi* are in poetry what the dwarf or cripple is in human nature. Here again, by their acceptance of this halting meter, the Greeks displayed their acute aesthetic sense of propriety, recognizing the harmony which subsists between crabbed verses and the distorted subjects with which they dealt—the vices and perversions of humanity—as well as their agreement with the snarling spirit of the satirist."

There is an echo of this quote, one that Williams found relevant to his search for a new measure, in the final lines of Book 5, the last complete installment of *Paterson* (p. 236):

> We know nothing and can know nothing
> > but
>
> the dance, to dance to a measure
> contrapuntally,
> > Satyrically, the tragic foot.

This was not my first introduction to the Ephesian inventor of the "limping foot," who lived and made poems around 540 BC. I had read what remains of his work in a book by the late Finnish poet Pentti Saarikoski, a contemporary and a friend, who in 1959 published a collection of poems titled *Runot ja Hipponaksin runot* (*Poems and the Poems of Hipponax*). Saarikoski, one of the major European poets of the twentieth century—even though he was far from tame enough for "Nobels" or "MacArthurs"—was also a prolific translator from classical Greek as well as from modern classics, including Joyce's *Ulysses.* While he went on later to write two powerful postmodern "epics"

(*What Is Really Going On* and *Trilogy*), in his 1959 volume he demonstrated his interest in how brief a poem may get and still be a poem—whether its brevity is due to the ravages of time (as in the case of many ancient Greeks) or to the author's desire to explore the possibilities of the laconic.

No "complete" poem by Hipponax survives. All we have is ninety-two mostly short quotes, in the works of later authors on history and its metrics and mores, chosen for being exemplary in one way or the other. Obviously, a fragment that was chosen as a "technically interesting" example of Hipponax's "lame or limping foot," the *choliamb,* may lose much of its raison d'être in translation:

> what a mob

or

> libations and innards of a wild sow

may not seem all that evocative, or merely evocative, hovering just below the threshold of "interesting." One might say that "The Collected Poems of Hipponax" as they can be found in the Loeb Classical Library's *Herodes, Cercidas, and the Greek Choliambic Poets (Except Callimachus and Babrius),* edited and translated by A. D. Knox, late fellow of King's College, Cambridge (1926), are an aleatory (or "stochastic") work composed by Clio, Muse of History, employing her own secret chance operations formula, in a tradition later brought to full bloom by John Cage and Jackson Mac Low, and also in "cut-ups" in the related lineage of Tristan Tzara, William S. Burroughs, and Brion Gysin.

The arrangement of the fragments in the Loeb edition is chronological, i.e., in the order of the approximate dates of the extant papyri and other texts in which lines attributed to Hipponax appear. Saarikoski's Finnish versions follow this arrangement fairly closely. I have created an "intuitive" display of the pieces, consisting of four parts (or poems, if you wish), under the headings:

"Careless Love" (check out Dr. John's recorded version of that American classic)

"What a Mob" (consisting of angry, vicious, and slanderous material)

"Screech Screech Here Come the Ghosts" (Or, "People Who Died") (see Ted Berrigan's poem, Jim Carroll's song)

"Still Waiting for My Winter Coat" (lines dealing with the ever-present needs and wishes of the unhoused and impecunious)

The four sections reflect what little is known about the poet's life.

From Pliny the Elder's *Natural History* we learn, in a passage dealing with the annals of Greek sculpture, that Hipponax was a satirical poet of Ephesus (c. 540 BC) who became involved in a feud with the sculptor Bupalos. The reason for this feud seems to have been a woman, Arété, whose affections Bupalos alienated from Hipponax. Either before or after (we don't know) Arété rejected Hipponax for Bupalos, the latter created a three-dimensional caricature of the poet, presumably in marble or some other stone. One wishes this piece of sculpture had survived; in Mary Renault's novel *The Praise Singer* (1978), a fictional autobiography of Hipponax's far more successful contemporary Simonides, we find the following description of the poet's appearance:

"He limped in one leg, which he had broken as a child, so that it was shorter than the other. The foot turned in, and his rocking gait had twisted his whole body, making his shoulders tilted. I thought it no wonder he should be bitter, for princes would not want to see him about their courts . . . That his clothes were dirty, I put down to his having no wife; but I thought that in a city not short of water, he could have washed himself. He ate noisily, and was helped twice." (p. 38)

Here, the "limping" measure is understood as the poet's translation of his physical handicap into a new poetics.

Whether or not Hipponax was physically repulsive and unsanitary, he certainly often found others to be so. He became notorious for his irreverent and slanderous verses, and after Ephesus became a Persian colony (presumably when Hipponax was still young and feisty), the new vice-regents of the city found him undesirable and politically incorrect and banished him:

"He did not go far, just north across the headland to Klazomenai. Now and then we would get news of him, or someone would bring back one of his poems . . . They grew more savage; we heard rumors of someone he'd caused to hang himself. He did not live very well, however, and came down to cadging from strangers in the harbor, or begging alms from people whose enemies he had reviled. He died, they say, lying in rags in the marketplace . . . One or two citizens, I've heard, poured oblations upon his grave, thinking his spirit would do mischief if not appeased." (*The Praise Singer*, p. 41)

"Careless Love" is the tale of Hipponax's infatuation with Arété, her rejection of him in favor of the sculptor Bupalos, and his subsequent indulgence in negative emotions. In "What a Mob" we see scattered 2,400-year-old reflections from Hipponax's verbal laser beams as they were aimed at dribblers, gluttons, imitators of Homer, corrupt judges, dumb painters, witches, sadists, masochists, con-men . . . "Screech Screech Here Come the Ghosts" is a similarly patchy frieze of elegiac matter. "Still Waiting for My Winter Coat" gathers the ancient street poet's prayers, complaints, and curses, echoed later in the works of François Villon and our own Charles Bukowski. Pentti Saarikoski, in notes to his translation, mentions Callimachus and Catullus as poets who regarded Hipponax as a master (and presumably still had access to a body of his recorded work).

Knox's and Saarikoski's translations have served as source texts for these versions. Like Saarikoski (who cites the Knox edition), I have tried my best not to stray too far from Knox's post-Victorian literalness, while also relying on Saarikoski's knowledge of classical Greek to guide me. Since mine is not a scholarly translation, more like a transcription—or if you wish, a "version,"—I refrain from encumbering it with footnotes.

While giving Hipponax my best shot, I have sometimes wondered what on earth compelled me to engage with this oh-so-long-dead (white? probably coppery, and certainly ornery) male who was so obviously of the slash-and-burn persuasion in his private/political life and work, yet prone to feeling sorry for himself; whom Mary Renault suspects of having provided such eloquent negative poetic testimony on the character of one of his enemies that the latter was scapegoated by the citizens, not a pleasant process; who sounds as if he didn't like his species fellows very much—any more than they cared for him—?

The answer is, I think, simply that "Now and then . . . someone would bring back one of his poems" from his ragged exile at Klazomenai, and that in the twentieth century, now half a century ago, an admired and beloved friend (whose own life was not lacking in Hipponactean themes) brought what is left of them to my attention. Then, there was that intriguing quote in *Paterson* by William Carlos Williams, whose understanding of American idiom and measure went far beyond the literal.

I Careless Love

on my way to Arété I saw
the heron fly just right

"all right all right all right"
I thought

and I did stay with her
all night

*

lamp-
light on her face

above mine

*

her slave stumbled and broke
the cup so we drank from a

bucket   I had the first drink
then Arété   downed the rest

*

baked goods from Amathusa
bread from Cyprus a bucket

of honey (a gift from the flower-
eaters) sweet Rhodian

ointment a garland of damson
flowers & mint aahh mmm

*

pierced the stopper
with a thin tube

*

soothed
my nostrils

(peanut oil)

*

greased
my keel

*

her lips
voracious

as a heron's beak

*

I love you more than I
love anyone else I swear

this to you by this
head of cabbage

*

silky
slit

*

stepping
proudly

like an
arch-

necked
horse

*

o but why did you take to your bed
that arsehole Bupalos?

*

man carved out of stone

*

threatens to render me senseless

*

told them to punch Hipponax in the mouth
told them to throw rocks at Hipponax

*

got away thanks to the seven-
leaf cabbage (Pandora's offering
at the Thargelia before *she* copped it)

*

here hang on to my shirt
while I bop Bupalos right

in the eye for I am ambi-
dextrous and my aim is

perfect

*

thought it was him
so let him have it

*

ripped his cloak
slashed him
down the middle

*

she rents out her tongue
for eighty bucks

*

you want her?
I'll let you have her

dirt cheap
her nose a bell
with snot for a clapper

why bother to wrap it up
(it isn't fresh partridge, exactly)

*

another game?
with those loaded dice?

you must be kidding

*

no more warming your
chilblains at my embers

*

so   fooling The In-Bred of Erythrea
Bupalos feeds at the trough

(Arété
beside him)

*

then they shrieked at each other

*

hips out of whack
no teeth only one eye

she sure knows how to pick 'em

*

may Artemis strike you down
or Apollo

(I don't care)

II   What a Mob

when they catch Phrygians
the Soloeci sell them to Miletus

where they need slaves for their mills

*

what a mob

*

was that a fart or a croak?

*

they drool
like a sieve

*

Kikon you hideous glutton son
of Amythaon your head may be

crowned with bay leaves but your
forecast doesn't look good

*

starve him and whip his gonads
pelt him with rocks in the meadow

beat him with twigs like a scapegoat

*

hold it Mimnes I don't think it is
such a good idea to paint the snake

on the side of that trireme with its
tail at the prow its head at the stern

if the snake bites his leg the brawny
helmsman will roar "count me out"

*

galloping upsidedown you lay there
after she snipped the cord

*

sing Muse of Mrs. Eurymedontiades
who needs no cutlery to wolf her food

shout Rabble vote for her death by stoning
by the Sea ever-restless

*

a hypocrite
the judge who condemned you
a paterfamilias
smirking at whores

*

with three witnesses he returned
to the bootlegger's place and found

84

a man who having no broom was busy
sweeping the floor with a broomstick

*

then she said in a strange tongue
now I'll clean your disgusting

arsehole she beat me with twigs
like a scapegoat caught between

two boards I hung above dung
beetles came to the feast

*

(handy invective)

one who barfs at the feast
old sow fed on slops

cow pie's sister
Ephesian porker

bag of puréed squid

III   Screech Screech Here Come the Ghosts
(Or, "People Who Died")

screech screech
here come the ghosts

*

Myson whom Apollo
called the wisest of all

*

pillaged along the road to Smyrna
through Lydia past the burrow of Alyattes

past Gyges' grave mound past
Ardys' splendid slab and Sadyattes' tomb

the mighty conqueror
his belly pointing west

*

his chariot powered by white stallions from Thrace
he charged the walls of Troy and was slain

*

a better judge than Bias from Priene

*

bright Cybebe
Bendis from Thrace

daughters of Zeus

*

he lived in Smyrna
the wrong side of town

halfway to Hades

*

and how did he get to Kypsos

*

libations and innards of a wild sow

*

black fig-tree

*

sister of the vine

*

clean cock and balls

*

happy the hunter

IV   Still Waiting for My Winter Coat

called on Hermes
strangler of dogs

brother of thieves
a.k.a. Kandaules

(in Scythia):
PLEASE HELP ME OUT

                        *

ah . . . to wear a mantle
of mountain sheep's wool . . .

Hermes lord of Cyllene
great son of Maia

Hipponax begs you:
send me a winter coat

                        *

for I am starving

                        *

unfunny he who drinks his lunch

                        *

now that was good advice

                        *

last night while I lay sleeping
someone made off with my clothes

lay in a room on a pallet buck naked

*

o teeth
you

that used to reside
in my jaw

*

picked tarragon out of a dented bucket
hands shook trembled

like the toothless
when the north wind blows

*

Zeus
Emperor of Olympus

Big Daddy

*

no scrumptious feast of partridge and hare
no sesame pancakes

no fritters drenched
in honey

nor yummy Lebedian figs
from far-off Kamandolos

*

for Hipponax:

    1 coat
    1 shirt

    1 pair of sandals
    1 pair of winter shoes

        (and 60 gold bars
        to hide in the wall)

*

still waiting for my shaggy greatcoat
to keep me from freezing in winter

and for that pair of winter shoes
to save my poor feet from chilblains

*

Plutos must have gone blind
he's never found his way to my house to tell me

90

"greetings dear Hipponax
see here I brought you this bag of silver"

*

o great Athena
please grant me a gentle master

one who won't beat me

*

I bow to Hermes
wait for the sun to rise

*

in his bright shirt

Coffee House Press began as a small letterpress operation in 1972 and has grown into an internationally renowned nonprofit publisher of literary fiction, essay, poetry, and other work that doesn't fit neatly into genre categories.

Coffee House is both a publisher and an arts organization. Through our *Books in Action* program and publications, we've become interdisciplinary collaborators and incubators for new work and audience experiences. Our vision for the future is one where a publisher is a catalyst and connector.

Funder Acknowledgments

Coffee House Press is an internationally renowned independent book publisher and arts nonprofit based in Minneapolis, MN; through its literary publications and *Books in Action* program, Coffee House acts as a catalyst and connector—between authors and readers, ideas and resources, creativity and community, inspiration and action.

Coffee House Press books are made possible through the generous support of grants and donations from corporate giving programs, state and federal support, family foundations, and the many individuals who believe in the transformational power of literature. This activity is made possible by the voters of Minnesota through a Minnesota State Arts Board Operating Support grant, thanks to the legislative appropriation from the arts and cultural heritage fund and a grant from the Wells Fargo Foundation Minnesota. Coffee House also receives major operating support from the Amazon Literary Partnership, the Bush Foundation, the Jerome Foundation, the McKnight Foundation, Target, and the National Endowment for the Arts (NEA). To find out more about how NEA grants impact individuals and communities, visit www.arts.gov.

Coffee House Press receives additional support from the Alexander Family Foundation; the Archer Bondarenko Munificence Fund; the Elmer L. & Eleanor J. Andersen Foundation; the David & Mary Anderson Family Foundation; the Buuck Family Foundation; the Carolyn Foundation; the Dorsey & Whitney Foundation; Dorsey & Whitney LLP; the Knight Foundation; the Matching Grant Program Fund of the Minneapolis Foundation; the Schwab Charitable Fund; Schwegman, Lundberg & Woessner, P.A.; the Scott Family Foundation; the US Bank Foundation; VSA Minnesota for the Metropolitan Regional Arts Council; the Archie D. & Bertha H. Walker Foundation; and the Woessner Freeman Family Foundation.

The Publisher's Circle of Coffee House Press

Publisher's Circle members make significant contributions to Coffee House Press's annual giving campaign. Understanding that a strong financial base is necessary for the press to meet the challenges and opportunities that arise each year, this group plays a crucial part in the success of Coffee House's mission.

Recent Publisher's Circle members include many anonymous donors, Mr. & Mrs. Rand L. Alexander, Suzanne Allen, Patricia A. Beithon, Bill Berkson & Connie Lewallen, the E. Thomas Binger & Rebecca Rand Fund of the Minneapolis Foundation, Robert & Gail Buuck, Claire Casey, Louise Copeland, Jane Dalrymple-Hollo, Jennifer Kwon Dobbs & Stefan Liess, Mary Ebert & Paul Stembler, Chris Fischbach & Katie Dublinski, Kaywin Feldman & Jim Lutz, Sally French, Jocelyn Hale & Glenn Miller, the Rehael Fund-Roger Hale/Nor Hall of the Minneapolis Foundation, Randy Hartten & Ron Lotz, Jeffrey Hom, Carl & Heidi Horsch, the Amy L. Hubbard & Geoffrey J. Kehoe Fund, Kenneth Kahn & Susan Dicker, Stephen & Isabel Keating, Kenneth Koch Literary Estate, Jennifer Komar & Enrique Olivarez, Allan & Cinda Kornblum, Leslie Larson Maheras, Jim & Susan Lenfestey, Sarah Lutman & Rob Rudolph, the Carol & Aaron Mack Charitable Fund of the Minneapolis Foundation, George & Olga Mack, Joshua Mack, Gillian McCain, Mary & Malcolm McDermid, Sjur Midness & Briar Andresen, Maureen Millea Smith & Daniel Smith, Peter Nelson & Jennifer Swenson, Marc Porter & James Hennessy, Jeffrey Scherer, Jeffrey Sugerman & Sarah Schultz, Nan G. & Stephen C. Swid, Patricia Tilton, Stu Wilson & Melissa Barker, Warren D. Woessner & Iris C. Freeman, Margaret Wurtele, and Joanne Von Blon.

For more information about the Publisher's Circle and other ways to support Coffee House Press books, authors, and activities, please visit www .coffeehousepress.org/support or contact us at info@coffeehousepress.org.

LITERATURE
is not the same thing as
PUBLISHING

Also by Anselm Hollo

Corvus
Guests of Space
Notes on the Possibilities and Attractions of Existence
Outlying Districts
Pick Up the House

The Tortoise of History was designed by
Bookmobile Design & Digital Publisher Services.
Text is set in Minion Pro.